THE FOOD CHAIN VS. THE FOOD WEB

FROM SIMPLE TO COMPLEX SYSTEMS

Children's Nature Books

BABY PROFESSOR
EDUCATION KIDS

Speedy Publishing LLC
40 E. Main St. #1156
Newark, DE 19711
www.speedypublishing.com

Are you curious to know the difference between the food chain and the food web?

All living animals and plants need energy for survival. Plants depend on water, soil, and the sun for it, while animals depend on plants, as well as animals for it. In this book we will be covering both subjects and how they work in order for plants and animals to live.

Animals and plants rely on each other for survival in an ecosystem. This is often referred to as the food web or food chain.

Food chain.

Zebra herd on African savanna at sunset.

WHAT IS A FOOD CHAIN?

How different organisms survive by eating each other is known as a food chain, starting with a plant and then ending with an animal. An example would be writing the chain for a lion as follows: grass $\longrightarrow$ zebra $\longrightarrow$ lion. The lion eats the zebra, which eats the grass.

ocean surface – 0 m

Epipelagic zone

about 200 m

Mesopelagic zone

about 1 000 m

Bathypelagic zone

about 4 000 m

Abyssopelagic zone

ocean floor

Hadopelagic zone

The diversity of wildlife in the oceanic zones.

LINKS OF
THE CHAIN

The links are named by description and depend on what the organism eats and how it is able to contribute to the ecosystem's energy.

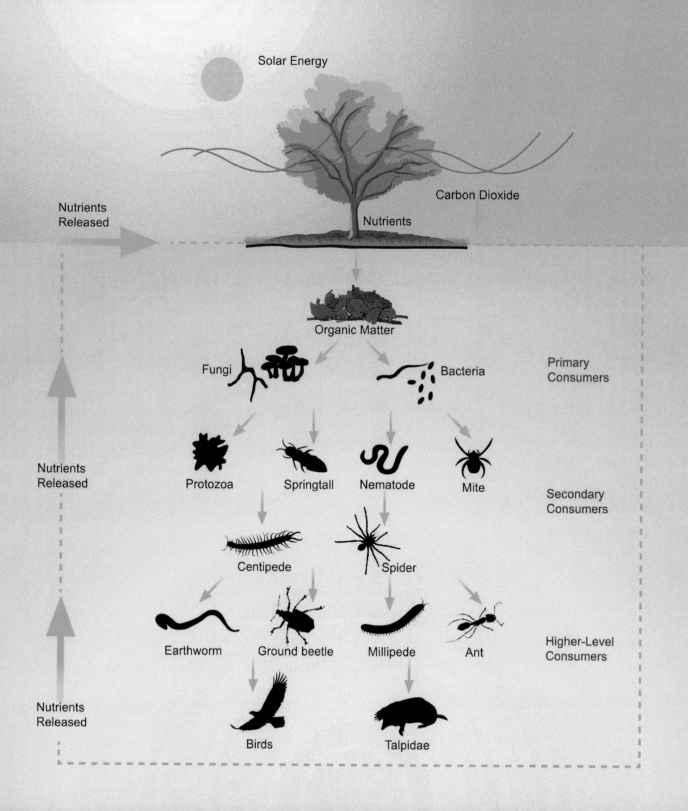

PRODUCERS - Plants are considered to be producers since they are able to produce the energy needed by the ecosystem. They are able to do this since they absorb it from the sun by a process known as photosynthesis. In addition, they have to have water and nutrients provided from the soil. However, plants are the only organism that can create new energy.

The soil food web is the community of organisms living all or part of their lives in the soil. It describes a complex living system in the soil and how it interacts with the environment.

In a marine ecosystem, the plant-like organisms known as algae dominate the producers. It can be tiny, such as diatoms, or can be very large, similar to giant kelp which can be found off of the California coast. In either instance, oceans are a great spot for producers. Since Earth is covered by 72 percent water, it makes sense that a lot of the oxygen found on Earth comes from our oceans.

View of tropical rocky beach landscape with green seaweed.

Another ecosystem that contains several producers is the rainforest. While they cover only approximately six percent of Earth's surface, they are able to produce almost 40 percent of the oxygen because of the amount of plants that live there.

Since oceans and rainforests are plentiful in numbers of producers, there are several webs existing in each of these ecosystems. The algae and plants provide the energy for a lot of the creatures that live there.

Tropical dense cloud forest covered in fog, Central Africa.

Plant-eating animals are known as herbivores or primary consumers. In many instances, primary consumers are also referred to as prey species since they often get eaten by different animals. They do not produce any energy, they only use it. Primary consumers that live on land include antelope, deer, mice, chipmunks, insects, birds, horses and elephants. Marine primary consumers include several species of fish, zooplankton, sea urchins, snails and krill.

Chipmunk eating pine nuts.

Animals eating other animals are known as carnivores or secondary consumers. They eat meat and often are referred to as predatory since they hunt for their prey. Terrestrial secondary consumers include spiders, wolves, coyotes, hyenas, hawks, snakes and lions. Marine secondary consumers include sea turtles, sea anemones, sea stars, lobsters, sharks, bluefish and killer whales.

Barn owl with mouse prey.

Secondary consumers also obtain energy from the sun, even though it is indirectly. The secondary consumers eat the primary consumers who ate the producer. As a result of this process, the secondary consumer obtains less energy than that of the primary consumer.

Because of the ten percent rule, the energy available for the secondary consumer is about one percent of the original amount of energy received from the sun. Thus, the secondary consumers need to eat larger prey or eat more often to meet their energy needs.

Wolf at meal time.

DECOMPOSERS – An organism that eats decaying matter (dead animals and dead plants) is known as a decomposer. Decomposers consist of, but they are not limited to, fungi, bacteria and worms. This helps to put the nutrients back into the soil for the plants to survive on.

If we return to this example: grass ⟶ zebra ⟶ lion; grass is the producer, zebra is the primary consumer, and the lion is the secondary consumer.

Closeup of an earthworm in the dirt.

Impala herd stampeding past Zebras.

ENERGY LOST

As we discussed earlier, energy in the food chain is created from the plants, or producers, which convert the light from the sun into energy using the process of photosynthesis. The remaining food chain only uses energy. Less and less energy becomes available as you go through the chain. Because of this, there are less organisms the further you get along the food chain.

In the example on the previous page, grass is more abundant than zebras, and there are more zebras than there are lions. The lions and the zebras use energy by running, breathing and hunting.

Lion hunting zebra.

EACH LINK PLAYS AN IMPORTANT ROLE

Links that are higher up in the chain depend on the lower links. While lions do not eat grass, they would not survive long if there was not any grass since the zebras would then have nothing to eat.

Giraffe and zebras.

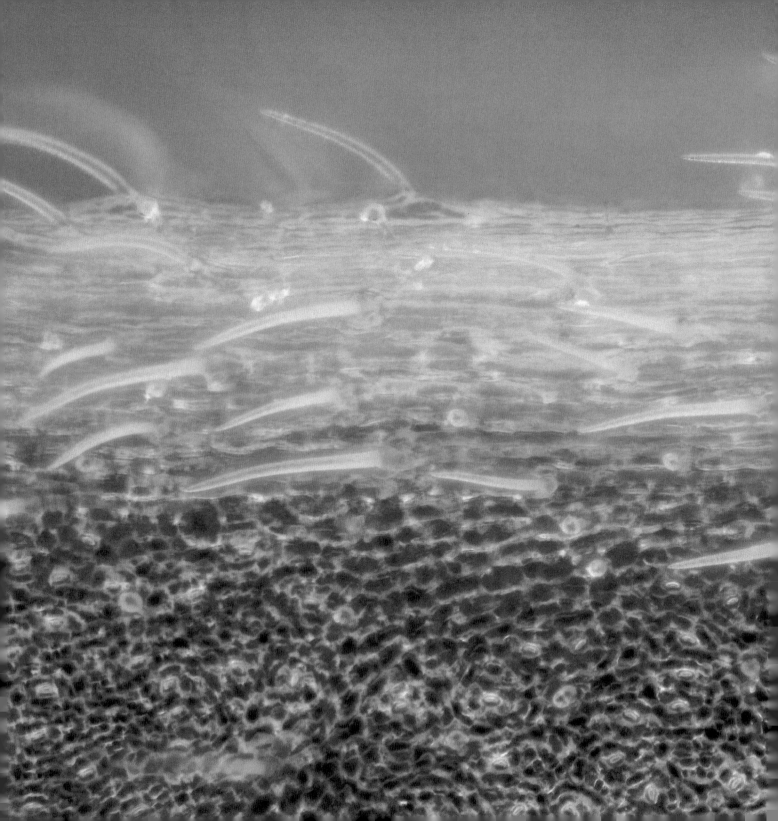

Extreme magnification - Vein on a leaf covered with hairs.

WHAT IS PHOTOSYNTHESIS?

In order to survive, plants need three basics: carbon dioxide, sunlight and water. They breathe carbon dioxide similar to how we breathe oxygen. As plants breathe in carbon dioxide, they then breathe out oxygen.

They are a great source of oxygen on Earth and help to keep us living. Now that we know plants use sunlight for energy, they obtain water from the rain, and get carbon dioxide from breathing, this process is known as photosynthesis -- taking these three ingredients and creating food.

The photosynthesis process.

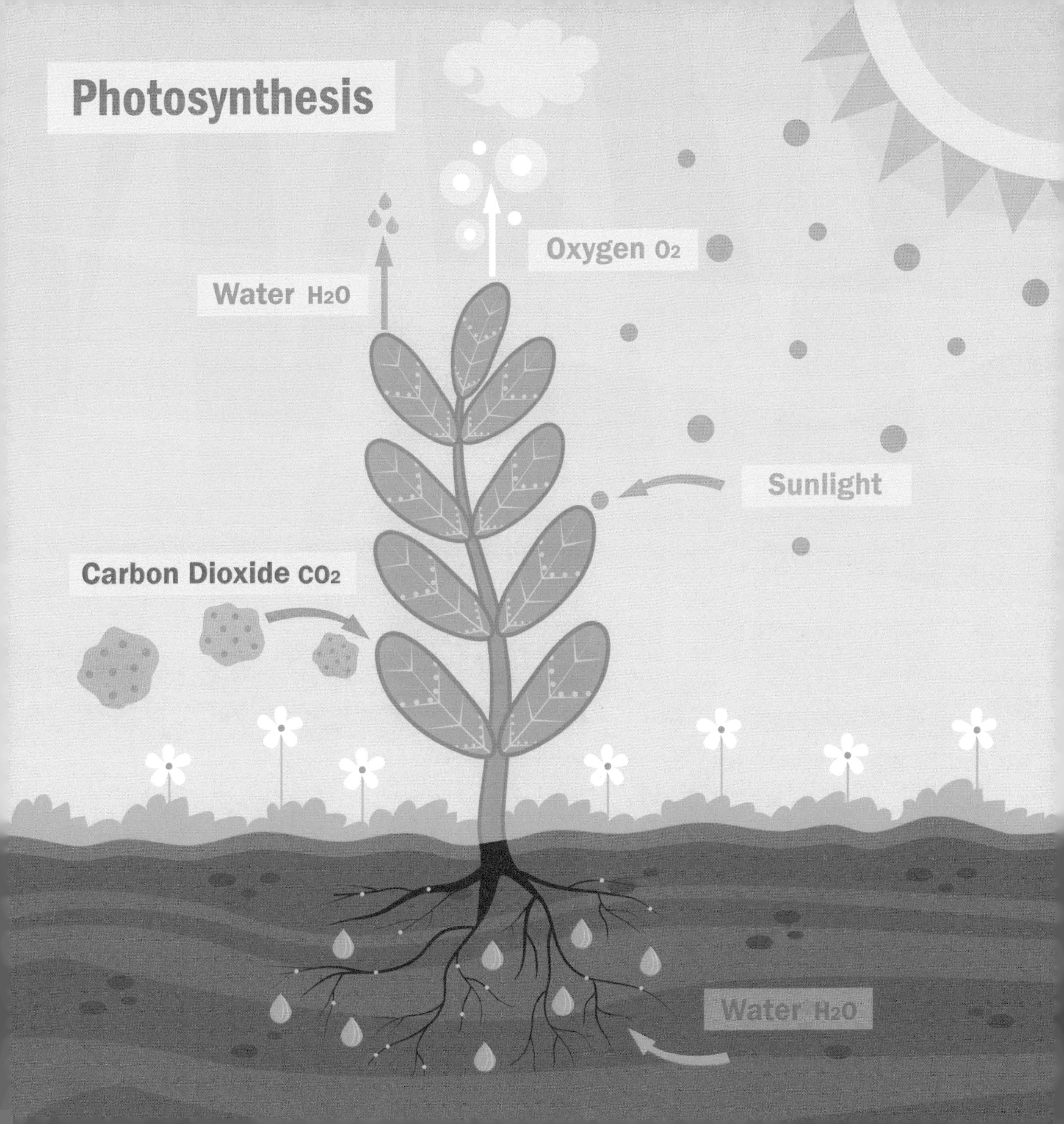

Photosynthesis

Water H_2O

Oxygen O_2

Sunlight

Carbon Dioxide CO_2

Water H_2O

Praying mantis having meal.

THE FOOD WEB

All types of life need energy to survive. Whether it is a living organism that makes it, or if they get it from food they hunt, it is necessary to keep and maintain their bodies. Metabolism, cell division, growth, hunting and reproduction are processes that all require energy.

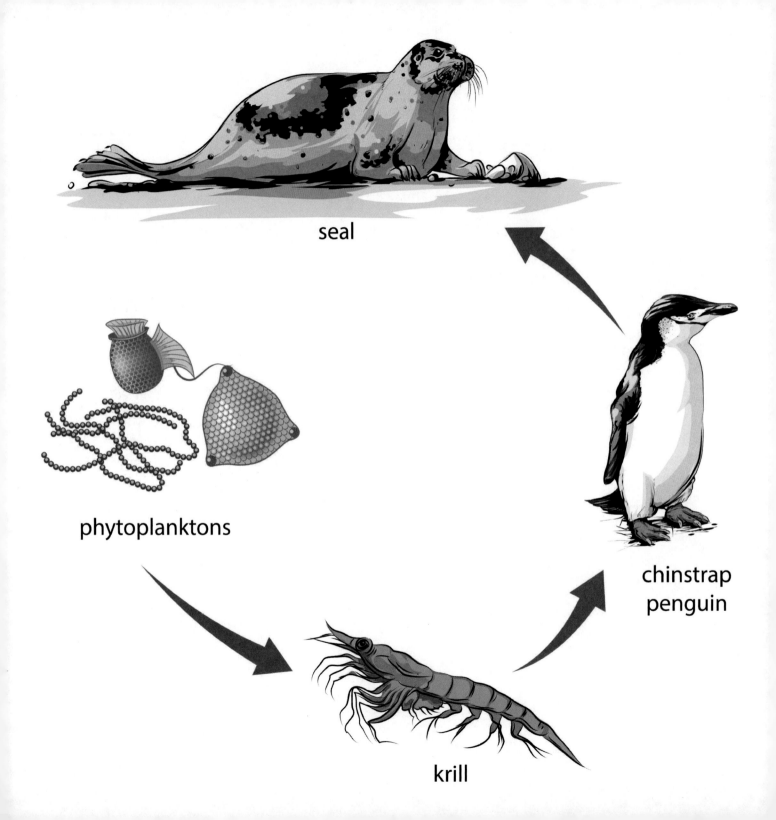

seal

phytoplanktons

chinstrap
penguin

krill

The ultimate source is the sun. If we did not have the sun, nothing would survive. Because of this, living things have created unique ways for harnessing this energy and using it for their well-being. Special relationships have developed and interactions allowing the transference of energy. Once captured, it is passed through the many organisms in a certain area. This transference is referred to as a food web.

Antarctic food chain.

Food webs, in their most simple form, are created by chains. As discussed earlier, the direct transfer of energy between the organisms is known as the food chain. This might be as simple as a mouse eating seeds on the floor of the forest.

Then, here comes a snake that eats that mouse. Later on, the snake is eaten by an owl. With each of these steps, some of the sun's energy, which can be found in the seeds, is passed on.

Basic marine food chain.

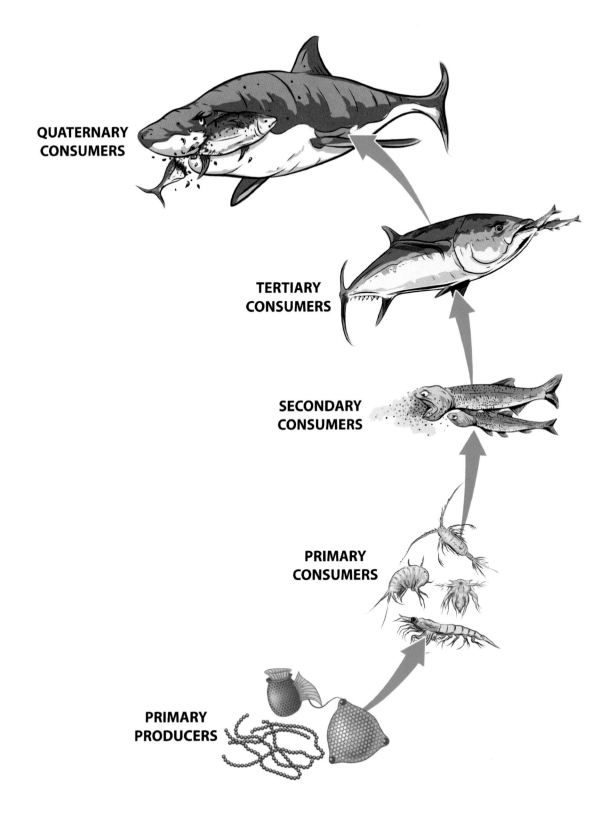

QUATERNARY CONSUMERS

TERTIARY CONSUMERS

SECONDARY CONSUMERS

PRIMARY CONSUMERS

PRIMARY PRODUCERS

The transfer of energy is not accurately portrayed in an ecosystem as a chain since there can be several organisms that can be consumed, and many that do the eating. The mouse referred to earlier might eat the seeds, but it might also eat berries, or even grass. This same mouse might then be eaten by the snake, the owl or possibly a fox.

North pole food chain example.

The owl might eat the snake, but the snake could also be eaten by a coyote or a fox. As each of these organisms can eat several things, and be eaten by several things, the food web is a more accurate representation about the transfer of energy.

Food chain.

TROPHIC LEVELS

Listed here are the five trophic levels which are sometimes used by scientists in describing each level of a food web:

Level 1 consists of plants, which are producers.

Level 2 consists of animals that eat plants, known as herbivores, as the primary consumers.

Level 3 consists of animals that eat herbivores, known as carnivores, as the secondary consumers.

Level 4 consists of animals that eat carnivores, also known as carnivores, as tertiary consumers.

Level 5 consists of animals referred to as apex predators. Nothing consumes animals at this level.

Bengal tiger (Panthera tigris tigris) on a tree.

FOOD CHAIN LENGTH

A metric used for quantifying the structu of the food web trophic is the food chain length. This is an additional way to describe food webs to measure the numbers of species which are encountered as nutrients or energy transfer from plants to predators. Depending upon the parameters being considered, there are many ways for calculation of the food chain length, including interaction, energy or connectance.

The chain length, in its most simple form, is the number of links from the trophic consumer and the web base. The mean length of the complete web is the average of all of the lengths in the food web.

In this basic predatory-pray illustration, a deer would be one step away from the plants that it eats (a chain length of 1) and the wolf that eats that deer is two steps away from the plants (a chain length of 2).

While you have read quite a bit about the food chain and the food web, there is so much more to learn. For additional information, go to your local library, research the internet, and ask questions of your teachers, family and friends.

Visit

BABY PROFESSOR
EDUCATION KIDS

www.BabyProfessorBooks.com

to download Free Baby Professor eBooks and view
our catalog of new and exciting Children's Books

Made in the USA
Middletown, DE
29 October 2020